A Marriage Made in Italy

Area Guide 3: Rome

Callie Copeman-Bryant

A Marriage Made Publications
www.amarriagemade.co.uk

First published 2007

ISBN: 978-1-84753-070-7

Front cover photo: The Campidoglio Wedding Hall – Michelangelo Staircase

Rome

Busy yet laid-back, modern yet ancient, fashionable yet historical, linked by teeming, congested boulevards and flower-filled, cobbled piazzas, "The Eternal City" is a heady mix of contradictions – a cheerful whirlpool that mixes together all the fashion and life of an up-to-date capital with a thousand historical monuments and a thousand more stories of intrigue and drama. A wedding here really is anything you want it to be. Civil and religious weddings are both well catered for: there are hundreds of churches, including the majestic Vatican which will have a special significance for those arranging a Catholic ceremony, while those of you arranging a civil wedding are in no danger of feeling short-changed with the choice of civil venues, all situated in beautiful historical buildings.

The Eternal City

Nearest Airports: Rome Ciampino; Rome Fiumcino (Leonardo da Vinci)

Served by: Air Berlin, Alitalia, American Airlines, British Airways, EasyJet, Ryanair

Flying time from London: Approx 2.5 hours

Best time to visit: The hottest and most uncomfortable period here falls between June and September. This may well be a draw for you, but even if you're tempted to visit in the soaring temperatures it is advisable to avoid August when virtually everything, including most businesses, shuts down and the locals head for the cooler coastal areas. In fact, many Romans will tell you that September and October are the most beautiful months, although winter in Rome, especially around the Christmas period, is particularly special with virtually guaranteed sunshine, moderate temperatures and the churches full of nativity scenes. The atmosphere in and around the Vatican at this time of year is incomparable.

Films to get you in the mood: Roman Holiday, La Dolce Vita, Only You, Three Coins in the Fountain

About this Book

Used in conjunction with *A Marriage Made in Italy: The Wedding Planning Guide*, this book provides you with comprehensive information and advice about getting married in Rome. In this particular guide, you'll find an overview of logistical information, descriptions of ceremony and reception venues, and a directory of wedding related suppliers specific to Rome; details of Italian legal requirements and in-depth logistical information can be found in *The Wedding Planning Guide*, which is relevant for all locations in Italy.

The hotels and restaurants featured in this guide were extensively researched in 2006 to ensure that only companies with the best reviews and reputations were approached for inclusion, and all reviewed venues in the series have been personally visited and verified. Of these, the companies featuring the "Top Pick" logo were felt to offer the very best in the area in terms of service, location and value for money, although do bear in mind that this book features just a selection of the venues available, and there are many other, excellent choices out there.

At the Spanish Steps

Orientation

Quick Venue Guide

Size of Party	Civil Venue	Religious Venue	Reception Venue
Up to 10	Villa Lais Campidoglio Wedding Hall Caracalla Wedding Hall	Chapel of the Chorus San Giorgio in Velabro Santa Maria in Aracoeli San Bartolomeo all Isola Sant'Andrea in Quirinale San Silvestro in Capite The Irish College St Patrick's Irish Church Santa Susanna Santa Maria in Cosmedin	Hotel Forum Rome Hotel Splendide Royal Palazza Ferrajoli Parco dei Principi El Toula
Up to 50	Campidoglio Wedding Hall Caracalla Wedding Hall	Chapel of the Chorus San Giorgio in Velabro Santa Maria in Aracoeli San Bartolomeo all Isola Santa Maria in Cosmedin Sant'Andrea in Quirinale San Silvestro in Capite The Irish College St Patrick's Irish Church Santa Susanna Santa Maria in Cosmedin	St. Regis Grand Hotel Forum Rome Hotel Splendide Royal Palazza Ferrajoli Parco dei Principi El Toula
Up to 100	None Available	Chapel of the Chorus S. Giorgio in Velabro San Bartolomeo all'Isola Sant'Andrea al Quirinale San Silvestro in Capite St Patrick's Irish Church Santa Susanna Santa Giovanni e Paolo	St. Regis Grand Hotel Splendide Royal Palazza Ferrajoli Parco dei Principi El Toula Druids Rock
100+	None Available	S. Maria in Trastavere St. Maria in Aracoeli Santa Sabina in Aventine Santa Susanna San Giovanni e Paolo St Patrick's Irish Church	St. Regis Grand Palazza Ferrajoli Parco dei Principi Druids Rock

Distances Matrix

Reception Venues Ceremony Venues	St. Regis	Hotel Forum	Splendide Royal	Palazzo Ferrajoli	Parco dei Principi	Toula	Druids Rock
Campidoglio	1.5	0.7	3.0	1.7	3.3	1.5	1.2
Caracalla	2.7	2.4	4.2	3.7	4.6	3.4	2.1
Villa Lais	3.4	3.4	4.7	6.8	5.0	6.2	3.0
Chapel of the Chorus (Vatican)	3.9	2.5	2.4	1.9	3.4	1.7	3.9
S. Maria Trastavere	2.7	1.9	3.7	2.6	4.6	2.4	2.5
S. Maria Aracoeli	1.5	0.7	3.0	1.7	3.3	1.5	1.2
S. Giorgio	2.2	1.2	3.9	2.7	5.0	2.5	1.9
S. Bartolomeo	2.5	1.4	3.1	2.0	4.0	1.7	2.4
S. Andrea	0.6	0.9	1.0	1.5	1.6	2.2	0.4
S. Sabina	2.5	1.5	4.2	3.0	5.3	2.8	2.1
S. Silvestro	0.6	1.2	0.5	0.8	1.6	1.4	0.7
Irish College	0.8	0.4	2.4	2.4	2.7	2.7	0.4
St Patrick's	0.6	1.7	0.7	1.7	1.1	2.4	1.2
S. Susanna	0.4	0.1	0.7	1.2	1.5	2.5	0.6
S. Maria Cosmedin	0.9	0.5	1.6	2.2	2.4	1.9	1.1
S. Giovanni e Paolo	2.1	1.4	4.0	4.3	4.4	4.1	1.7

All distances are given in miles and are an approximate guide only

Venue Map

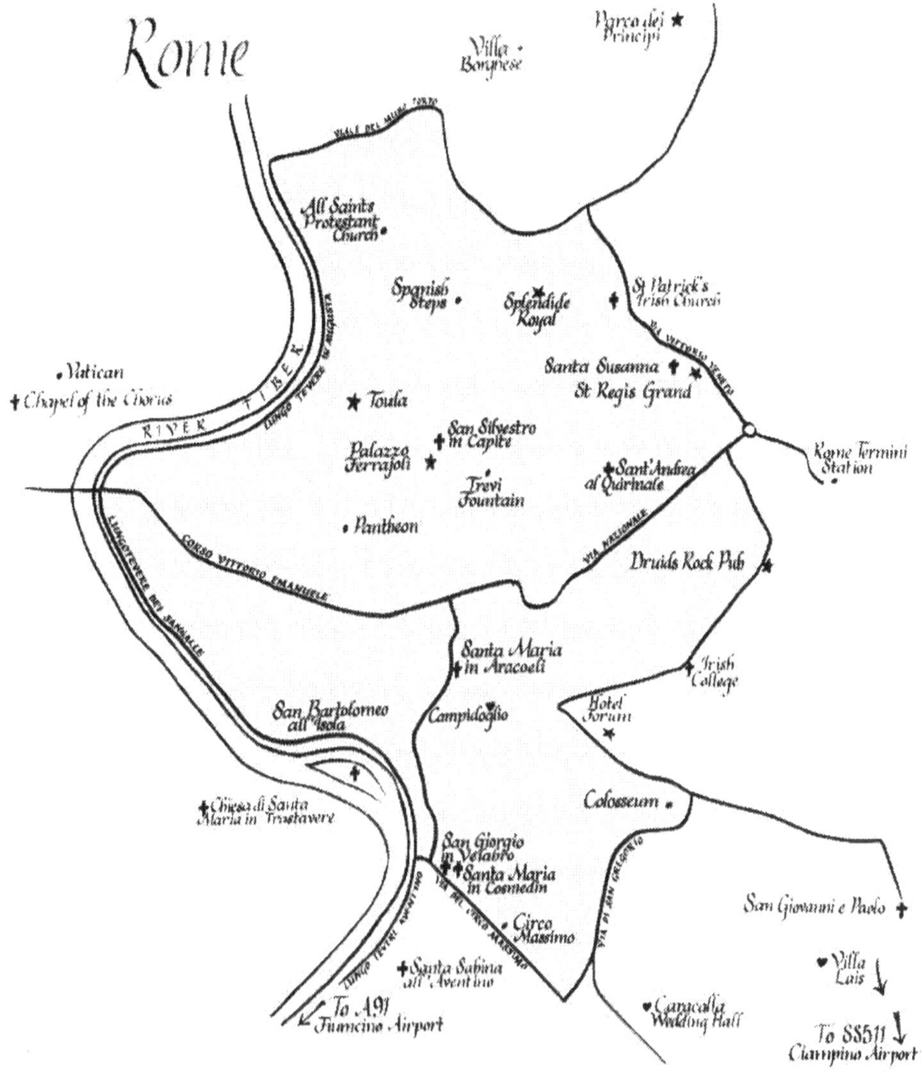

Intended as an approximate guide only. Not to scale.
Map provided by The Wedding Calligrapher.

♥ Civil Venue

✚ Religious Venue

★ Reception Venue

• Point of Interest

Planning a Wedding in Rome

As explained in Chapter 3 of *A Marriage Made in Italy: The Wedding Planning Guide*, there are very specific paperwork requirements that must be fulfilled before you can get married in Italy, and these requirements differ depending on your nationality. In most areas, the paperwork needed for your *Nulla Osta* (the all important Italian "No Impediment" Certificate, without which the wedding can't take place) can be completed just a few months before your wedding date, but in Rome the authorities require your paperwork to be in place before they will confirm your date, and all forms will need to have been submitted at least 16 weeks before the wedding. In the case of Catholic weddings, you will also need to abide by the regulations set by your parish and chosen ceremony church.

What follows is an outline of the steps you must take in order to fulfil the necessary requirements for civil and Catholic ceremonies in Rome, although don't forget that the rules are subject to change, and particulars vary between churches. In all cases you should seek confirmation of the requirements from your tour operator, co-ordinator or consular office. Further information about legal requirements can be found in Chapter 3 of *The Wedding Planning Guide*.

In order for the marriage to be legally binding, any person arranging a religious ceremony in Rome (excluding Catholic weddings held in Vatican City) must also follow the procedure for civil weddings; as Vatican City is a sovereign state, it is subject to slightly different regulations to the rest of Rome.

On a final note, if you're having a religious ceremony then before you go off on that all-important shopping trip, **check your venue's dress code**. Almost all churches will require you (and your guests) to have your shoulders and upper arms covered, so you may need to arrange a matching wrap or bolero if you're going for a strapless or strappy number.

Civil Weddings in Rome

Once you have followed the procedures outlined in Chapters 3 and 5 of *The Wedding Planning Guide*, your marriage banns will be posted at the relevant embassy in Rome for three weeks before the *Nulla Osta* is issued, after which you must contact the General Registry Office in Rome (the *anagrafe* in Via Petroselli) who will issue you with the relevant wedding paperwork. While you are there, you will need to swear a *giuramento* (an official oath) and have the *Nulla Osta* stamped with two *bolli* (stamps which you can buy from a tobacconist). Once stamped, the banns are posted in Piazza del Campidoglio and you will be able to make an appointment for the civil wedding. All these procedures will normally be handled for you by your co-ordinator or tour operator, if you have one.

Catholic Weddings in Rome

Under Italian law, the civil and religious aspects of religious weddings are considered separate, which means you must follow the civil procedure above in addition to the religious requirements. You should follow the procedures outlined in Chapters 3 and 5 of *The Wedding Planning Guide* and in addition to the documents specified, the bride and groom must provide two written statements confirming their freedom to enter into the marriage. All documents must be dated within six months of the ceremony date. During your first meeting with the priest you will complete a pre-nuptial enquiry form and go through the details of your *pre-cana*. Following this, all documents will be submitted by the priest to the local chancery for a *Nilhil Obstat* (or *Visum Est*). The Diocese of Rome requires all documents to be submitted one month in advance, but a wedding date at your chosen church can usually be provisionally booked before these steps have been completed. More information can be found at www.santasusanna.org or from www.irishcollege.org.

Catholic Weddings in Vatican City

As a sovereign state, the procedure for getting married in Vatican City differs slightly as the civil and religious requirements are combined, and not treated separately as they are elsewhere in Rome. The process can only be started between four and six months in advance of your preferred ceremony date, with that date only being set and confirmed once all paperwork is in place, a rigid procedure which leaves little time to make other arrangements. In general, the documentation submitted is the same as with any Catholic ceremony, the main difference being that you will not need to have your *Nulla Osta* stamped at the General Registry Office. More information can be found at www.santasusanna.org.

Anglican and Other Religious Weddings in Rome

Any non-catholic religious ceremony will not be considered legally binding, which means you will need to hold a civil ceremony before arranging a religious blessing. Further information on Anglican venues can be requested from www.allsaintsrome.org, or see http://roma.katolsk.no/non_catholic.htm for information on all other religious venues.

Civil Venues

Campidoglio Wedding Hall

If you want opulence, you can't get much better than the gilt-edged Campidoglio Wedding Hall, right in the historic centre of Rome, set on the calm, geometric Piazza del Campidoglio, high above the traffic on the Capitoline Hill overlooking the remains of the Roman Forum. Weddings take place inside the beautiful *Sala Rossa,* entered via the famous Michelangelo Grand Staircase which sweeps from the piazza, up the outside of the building directly to the first floor room, a spectacularly grand interior upholstered in wine and burgundy, all edged with gilt and surrounded by beautiful marble pillars and ornate chandeliers. After the ceremony it is customary to spend some time among the neighbouring ruins of the Forum for your wedding photographs.

As you can imagine, a setting such as this is extremely popular and so weddings here are notoriously brief, usually lasting no longer than 15 minutes. You can personalise the ceremony in small ways, but you'll be discouraged from making too many additions that are seen to take up time. Further details can be found at www.commune.roma.it/info_cittadino/schede/an_ma_03.htm

The Michelangelo Staircase, Campidoglio Wedding Hall

Caracalla Wedding Hall

The Caracalla Wedding Hall (*Complesso di Vignola Mattei*) appears to have extended the "red velvet and gilt edging" theme of the Campidoglio Wedding Hall, but this time it is set (somewhat at odds) inside an ancient stone church on a shady street by the grounds of the Roman Caracalla Baths. The 8th century venue is dark and cool, quiet and peaceful, and has an earthy, rustic feel to it. It has no decoration, but is extremely atmospheric with its austere, crumbling stone walls and brick arches. As demand for this venue is less than for the Campidoglio Wedding Hall, you will have more of an opportunity to linger over your ceremony in a quieter, more private setting, surrounded by peaceful parkland near the Circo Massimo. This venue holds around 50 guests, and weddings are celebrated on all week-days.

Caracalla Wedding Hall

Villa Lais
If the idea of getting married surrounded by bright, colourful art tempts you, then take a look at Villa Lais, a small civil venue set in villa parkland just outside the centre of Rome. The main Villa building hosts a citizens' advice and family centre, but attached is the charming, circular-shaped, 19th century chapel which provides an intimate venue for up to 30 guests. It features marble carvings and dazzling Renaissance frescoes which cover the walls and ceiling. For more information, go to
www2.comune.roma.it/villalais/home/home.html

Inside Villa Lais

Villa Lais

------------------------------ *Religious Venues* ------------------------------

Catholic Venues

Would you believe me if I told you there aren't many Catholic wedding venues available in Rome? No, you're right, and I'm not even going to try although, it has to be said, covering all the available churches in Rome would be as ridiculous as covering none of them (there are more than 900), so here is just a selection:

Chapel of the Chorus, St Peter's Basilica

First up is, of course, **St Peter's Cathedral** (*Basilica di San Pietro)* in Vatican City, the largest and most important Catholic church situated in the world's smallest state. The main body of the structure where the Pope celebrates Mass is as enormous as you would expect, but there are several smaller chapels on either side and it is in one of these, the **Chapel of the Chorus** (*Cappella del Coro)*, that wedding ceremonies take place.

Cappella del Coro

Entering the main cathedral, the chapel is situated on the left hand side of the nave (past two side altars and the crazily ornate baptismal font) and is entered through marble Corinthian pillars flanking wrought-iron gates normally closed against meandering sight-seers. It is filled with just the kind of splendour you'd expect - famous paintings and frescos by Michelangelo and Raphael cover the marble-sculpted walls, and the gilding is absolutely magnificent. Despite the ever-present curious tourists, it is a surprisingly private and intimate venue: during a wedding ceremony the gates are closed and heavy, velvet curtains are drawn across the entrance to give you the privacy and solemnity you need. The chapel can hold up to 80 guests, although fewer certainly wouldn't look amiss thanks to the layout of the room: wooden benches facing the altar hold around 30 to 40 people, while additional guests can be seated along the dark wooden choral benches on either side of the room. A singer and even the Pope's own organist are available to book at this splendid venue.

Inside the Vatican

The photo opportunities outside are equally outstanding, as the Basilica is situated on the world-famous piazza. Don't forget though that Vatican City is a sovereign state and the paperwork requirements differ slightly from the rest of Italy – contact the Vatican office or a local co-ordinator for full details. Ceremonies are celebrated every day of the week except for Wednesdays and Sundays, and are available at 10.30am only. Weddings are unavailable from December 18th to January 8th, during August, Holy Week, Easter Week and on various other holy days. The strict dress code dictates that shoulders, arms, back and legs must be covered. The fee for a wedding here is around €900.

If you do decide to get married at San Pietro, you may be interested to know that you can apply for newlywed tickets (*Sposi Novelli)* for the Pope's Audience - a special blessing held every Wednesday. Unfortunately individual blessings are no longer available, but it's still a great opportunity to take part in a very special event.

The Pope's Audience

Santa Maria in Trastavere
The interior of the 12th century Church of Santa Maria in the hip bohemian district of Trastevere is absolutely breath-taking and quite literally dazzling, as the focus here is on the heavily gilded apse and sparkling frescos, all offset by a beautiful white, green and red swirling mosaic floor. Thought to have been built on the site of the first official Christian church in Rome, the nave is flanked by numerous side altars, with granite Doric and Corinthian columns taken from the ruins of ancient Roman buildings, while overhead an astonishingly ornate ceiling consists of a sparking gold star and cross pattern. Outside, the church's simple façade is decorated with frescos and marble sculptures, and sits in front of a large open piazza edged with trendy pavement cafes and with a wonderfully ornate octagonal fountain at its centre, perfect for those wedding photos.

Santa Maria in Trastavere

Santa Maria in Aracoeli

Strictly for the fit and inadvisable in a hot, heavy wedding dress, the 12th century Church of Santa Maria in Aracoeli is set high on the Capitoline Hill and is reached by climbing over a hundred steps. The somewhat plain façade completely fails to prepare you for the splendour of the interior, which is adorned with thousands of colourful frescos and gilded paintings, surrounded by huge, carved columns and marble arches. Approaching the altar, one doesn't quite know where to look first: dozens of chandeliers surround the apse and fill the gaps between the Corinthian columns of the nave, while the splendid altar is full of paintings and icons in all the different colours of the rainbow - a colour scheme reminiscent of something you might see on your granny's fireplace back home. Red and gold chairs set on a red aisle carpet give the altar an additional sense of occasion for wedding ceremonies. The church can hold any size wedding party, as the main body of the building is huge and can hold well over 100 guests, whereas smaller weddings can be held at one of the side-altars if preferred.

Santa Maria in Aracoeli

San Giorgio in Velabro

The medieval church of San Giorgio is situated in the quiet area of Velabro, famous for its links with the ancient legend of Romulus & Remus. The church is a very popular wedding venue, and would be one to consider if you'd prefer to avoid the ostentatious feel of most other Roman churches as the interior is fairly plain, giving it an atmosphere of calm and serenity. In sharp relief to this austerity, however, is a wonderfully colourful frescoed apse and a beautiful, high medieval altar. The nave features white marble and granite Doric pillars, with a green aisle carpet covering the ancient stone floor. Although situated in a quiet side-street, this venue is just a short walk from the busy streets of Aventine and the River Tiber, so is deceptively central. The church is ideal for small weddings and will comfortably hold around 100 guests.

San Giorgio in Velabro

San Bartolomeo all Isola

One of the most romantic places in the city, the charming Tiber Island feels almost like a quaint village with its little cobbled streets and tiny street cafes. Here you can find the church of San Bartolomeo, an absolutely beautiful little church that holds around 70 guests. Friendly and intimate, the interior is wonderfully bright: stone Corinthian pillars topped with gold acanthus leaves line the nave in front of side altars where light streams in through tiny stained-glass windows, each altar filled with colourful, gilded frescos in sharp relief to the plain walls in between. The ceiling is a myriad of coloured geometric paintings, and the high altar is flanked by even more gilded frescos. This church is small but heart-stoppingly splendid, full of colour and interest, set on a small, picturesque piazza and with spectacular views of the river and the city beyond.

San Bartolomeo all Isola

Sant'Andrea in Quirinale

Just a short walk from the famous Trevi fountain in the district of Quirinale is the Church of Sant'Andrea, a Roman Baroque building designed by Bernini, who considered this to be his only perfect work. It certainly is very elegant – the church is set on a semi-circular set of steps featuring white Corinthian pilasters which frame an enormous doorway, a theme echoed in the interior Corinthian pillars which frame the magnificent altar. The main doors open directly into the oval shaped church - a cool, marble interior featuring dusky pink and white pilasters that flank six small side-altars. The architecture is astonishingly beautiful, with a black and white marble floor and a wonderfully ornate gold ceiling. High windows let an abundance of light onto the all-marble interior, where dozens of white cherubs hang around the acanthus leaves and peep down from the central dome. The apse features a huge painting of the crucifixion of St Andrew, surrounded by even more cherubs among gold roseate. When a wedding is taking place, a red velvet aisle carpet is laid, and red and gold chairs are set in front of the altar. This venue has a very cosy feel and, thanks to its shape, is perfect for very small weddings while comfortably holding up to 80 guests.

Sant'Andrea in Quirinale

Santa Sabina in Aventine

Built in the 5th century, the church of Santa Sabina high on the Aventine Hill looks very much as it did in those early days as it still has the huge windows that in other churches would typically have been walled-up in later restorations. Wonderfully light inside, the church has a gleaming white marble interior, Corinthian pillars, mosaic arches and a wooden ceiling that features a blue and gold star design, mirrored in the blue and gold chairs beneath. The apse behind the altar has a very unusual, extremely elegant dusky pink and white striped design which beautifully reflects the pillars of the nave and the geometric designs on the floor and ceiling. This church is very spacious and can comfortably hold up to 200 guests, but its vast size and layout would certainly make a smaller party feel less than cosy. Just outside the church is a small public garden which looks out across Rome towards Trastavere and the Vatican, and provides an ideal panorama for your wedding photos.

Santa Sabina in Aventine

San Silvestro in Capite

www.freewebs.com/saintsilvester

The first of four English language churches featured in this guide, the 12th century church of San Silvestro is a popular venue for English and Irish couples. The high altar, designed by Michelangelo, is situated in a colourful frescoed apse depicting the Baptism of Constentine, and the side-chapel of the church famously holds the relic of the head of John the Baptist. The interior of the church is ornately decorated and has particularly beautiful ceiling frescos.

San Silvestro is one of the most popular venues for English language weddings in Rome and as such the staff are well used to dealing with couples planning their weddings from overseas. Make sure you contact them well in advance of your wedding date in order to secure a booking here.

San Silvestro in Capite

The Irish College - Church of St John Lateran
www.irishcollege.org

If you'd like to take part in either a group wedding (Mondays) or be married by your own priest (Tuesdays to Fridays), then take a look at The Irish College, situated in the parish of St John Lateran. The nearby Basilica of St John of Lateran was the principal cathedral of the Catholic Church's former headquarters, and the church at the College (also known as the Church of St John Lateran) is particularly popular with Irish couples marrying in Rome.

This is a very friendly venue whose only real drawback is that you will have to take part in a group wedding unless you bring your own celebrant, as the College is unable to provide a celebrant for private weddings. The church also has a very plain interior, so bear this in mind if the promise of opulent interiors is what's drawing you to Rome.

The Irish College

St Patrick's Irish Church
www.stpatricksrome.com

The Irish Church of St Patrick was built in the 20th century on the site of Santa Maria in Posterula, whose frescos now adorn the walls of this new, neo-classical style church. Its altar is surrounded by marble alabaster pillars, pink granite columns, and a gilt mosaic apse.

This church is extremely popular with Irish couples, and is suitable for any size wedding party. During the summer months (excluding August and early September) the church offers group weddings only on Mondays, Tuesdays and Fridays. Out of season weddings are held on Mondays and Tuesdays, with Tuesdays being reserved for private weddings. For more information contact the Wedding Office which is open every week day from 8am to 9.30am, and from 4.30pm to 6.30pm (GMT).

St Patrick's Church

Santa Susanna

www.santasusanna.org

The seriously ornate American church of Santa Susanna is absolutely covered in frescos and decoration. It has an almost obscenely grand apse, a huge sweeping ceiling, and an abundance of gold-leaf covered marble carvings. Its high ceilings let in very little natural light, but the flickering candles create a calm, romantic atmosphere.

The church will seat around 100 guests, but it somehow has the feel of a much more intimate venue so a wedding with fewer guests wouldn't appear out of place. Situated between the Via Veneto and Piazza Republica, it is especially convenient for receptions at the St. Regis Grand Hotel, and is particularly popular with American couples.

Santa Susanna

Santa Maria in Cosmedin

Santa Maria in Cosmedin was first built in the 6th century and for centuries was primarily used by the Greek community. With a capacity for around 80 guests, it has a gothic styled interior and a medieval façade featuring the famous "Mouth of Truth" which, I should warn you, draws scores of chattering tourists who queue just outside the entrance to have their photo taken with the legendary biting beast. At the time of writing the church is closed for restoration, but by 2007 it should be open again and is well worth knowing about. I can't decide if this is romantic or not, but you might like to know that the high altar holds the skull of St Valentine which is crowned with roses every year on 14th February.

Santa Maria in Cosmedin

*Bocca della Verita -
The Mouth of Truth*

*Skull of
St Valentine*

Santi Giovanni e Paolo in Caracalla

Up a sweeping cobbled street next to the Roman Baths of Caracalla and situated in calm parkland is the church of San Giovanni e Paolo. A large church with carved marble pilasters and dozens of chandeliers, it has white and gold chairs, and high windows that let in plenty of natural light. The church seats around 150 guests.

Situated away from the historical centre and the famous city sights, this is a venue worth considering if you want to be married in calm surroundings rather than amid the bustle of city life.

San Giovanni e Paolo in Caracalla

Reception Venues

What follows is just a brief selection of reception venues covering a small variety of styles, budgets and locations. Almost all hotels and restaurants in Rome (of which there are hundreds) will cater for wedding receptions, so you shouldn't be dissuaded from searching for your own venues. Because there is such a myriad of hotels and venues to choose from in Rome, it's worth knowing that the luxury ones tend to be in the area east of Via del Corso heading towards Via Veneto, and in the area of the Spanish Steps, while other less expensive but very pleasant options can be found in Prati, Spagna or the trendy area of Trastavere.

Key to Price Guide

Please note all prices are approximate

€: Up to €50 per head
€€: €50 - €80 per head
€€€: €80 - €100 per head
€€€€: €100 - €150 per head
€€€€€: €150 - €200 per head
€€€€€€: Over €200 per head

St. Regis Grand Hotel €€€€€

Website: www.stregis.com/rome
Email: weddings.grandrome@stregis.com

"We got married at this hotel, and I could not say enough about the service and food… it certainly was a wedding to remember."

Rome Bride

Book the St. Regis Grand, and you'll feel like you've booked a reception venue and an event planner in one. The extraordinarily friendly staff at this polished old Grande Dame have developed a highly personalised wedding package that is unbeatable: hire of the venue comes with an experienced co-ordinator - a dedicated point of contact who will work with you on all aspects of planning your reception, and who will act as your on-the-day co-ordinator. The hotel has certainly put a great deal of thought into this package which not only reflects a real understanding of the challenges faced by couples planning their wedding in an overseas location, but also contains some lovely treats that include a complimentary first anniversary dinner at the hotel restaurant and pre-wedding spa treatments for the bride and groom. The event staff at the hotel are justifiably proud of their approach to managing receptions: their mission is to create an original event for each couple, so your event co-ordinator will work hard to establish the style and atmosphere you are aiming for and will tailor your event accordingly. It's safe to say that no two weddings here are alike, and you'll have a unique event planned exactly to your specifications.

The hotel was first converted from a monastery to a hotel in the late 1800s. Although it has recently undergone a full refurb, it still retains many of its original features and each function room is beautifully decorated in rich, warm colours. The rooms that will be allocated to your reception will depend on the number of guests: the magnificent **Ritz Ballroom**, with a capacity of 150 – 240, is reserved for larger receptions and features Murano glass chandeliers, mirrored walls, a bright frescoed ceiling and gleaming marble floor. The red and gold **Danieli** rooms can hold from 80 – 150 guests and have the additional attraction of a fragrant private garden filled with plants and statues, just perfect for pre-dinner drinks. The **Venezia** rooms, available for smaller receptions comprising 20 – 25 guests, feature wooden floors and large windows that let in plenty of natural light. These rooms are decorated in blue and gold, and are impeccable yet homely. Smaller receptions are also welcome at the hotel, although these will be held in the main restaurant.

The Ritz Ballroom, St. Regis Grand Hotel

Hairdressing and entertainment can be provided at a supplementary price, and the hotel has an in-house florist who can provide any floral displays you require. For entertainment, the hotel can arrange anything from musicians providing background music to theme nights, magicians, bands and discos.

Essential Information – St. Regis Grand Hotel:

Availability:	Open all year	Organisation:	A co-ordinator will be assigned to provide a one-to-one service and help you plan your event.
Size of party:	20 – 240	Entertainment:	Theme nights, discos and bands can be arranged, as well as background accompaniment. Loud music up to midnight only.
Children catered for:	Yes	Exclusivity:	It is highly unlikely that more than one reception would be held on the same day, although in this situation you would be kept informed and the events kept separate.

Prices from:	€160 per head.		
Price Includes			
Venue Hire	✓	Centre pieces	✗
Staff	✓	Wedding cake	✓
Meal (five courses)	✓	Entertainment	✗
Aperitifs & Canapés	✓	Table Wine	✓

Hotel Forum Rome €€€€
www.hotelforumrome.com

"I held my wedding reception here for 40 guests, on the rooftop terrace. I cannot recommend this hotel enough. The staff are excellent and cannot do enough to help, the food is to die for, the wedding cake magical and the overall ambience is fantastic."
Rome Bride

As the name suggests, this hotel is situated by the ruins of the Roman Forum, just a stone's throw from the Coliseum, the Campidoglio Wedding Hall and the Church of Santa Maria in Arecoeli. It has the lovely, polished walnut and leather interior of an old Bentley and the atmosphere of a gentleman's club, or even perhaps the first-class smoking room on board the Titanic. In any case, your gentlemen guests will look perfectly fitting taking a late port at the bar, while the Victorian styled sitting area, glossy wood fittings and ticking grandfather clocks combine to make a very plush setting for a drinks reception.

Rooftop Terrace, Hotel Forum Rome

The hotel offers just one option for your wedding breakfast, but it's a very worthy one. The rooftop restaurant - which overlooks the Forum ruins and has particularly stunning views by night - is cool, open and surrounded by bright, blooming window boxes. No separate function suite is available which means that, unless you have over 80 guests, you may well have to share the rooftop terrace with other hotel guests. However, the hotel is experienced in arranging wedding receptions and will endeavour to set your event apart by providing table decorations and all the space you need. The restaurant offers either a sit-down or buffet service, can supply all kinds of wedding cakes, and will decorate the tables with printed menus and floral arrangements to match your colour scheme. The menu is flexible and the hotel is more than happy to offer alternative selections.

Essential Information – Hotel Forum Rome:

Availability:	Open all year	Organisation:	Weddings receptions will be organised by the manager of the restaurant. The Maitre d' can assist with any additional bookings.
Size of party:	Up to 80	Entertainment:	Music permitted for evening receptions only. A small live band can be arranged for around €300. Couples may also bring their own CDs.
Children catered for:	Yes	Exclusivity:	Hire of the terrace is exclusive only for parties of over 80. Smaller groups will share the terrace with hotel guests, but the hotel only ever caters for one wedding reception at a time.

Prices from:	€120 per head		
Price Includes*			
Venue Hire	✓	Centre pieces	✓
Staff	✓	Wedding cake	✓
Meal (four courses)	✓	Entertainment	✓**
Aperitifs & Canapés	✓		

* Prices dependent on number of guests. Some charges apply for parties under 20.

**Depending on type of music requested. Live band costs around €300.

Hotel Splendide Royal €€€€
www.splendideroyal.com/salsa/en/index.html

"The absolute highlight was dinner at the rooftop restaurant, Mirabelle… the food was outstanding, and the views of the city were unbelievable."

Rome Honeymooner

There are many advantages to this venue, situated next to the park of *Villa Borghese* and just a few minutes away from the Spanish Steps. Not only is the hotel décor particularly bridal, but the rooms seem to have been designed with the bride and groom in mind. Part of an old monastery building, the rooms maintain many of the original trappings and all are wonderfully spacious, several with walk-in wardrobes that can be shut away from the rest of the room – a perfect feature for hiding that wedding dress. Most rooms have bathrooms with natural light, a distinct bonus if you are planning to have your hair and make-up done in your room, while some Superior bathrooms feature Jacuzzis and open out onto your own private terrace, providing you with the opportunity to start (or finish!) your wedding day in a wonderfully indulgent way.

The Terrace at Sunset, Hotel Splendide Royal

Superior rooms are very spacious, giving you plenty of room for your pre-wedding preparations and offering an intimate setting for a small hen-night get-together. If you and your fiancé would prefer a traditional night apart before the wedding but don't want the hassle of swapping rooms, the Presidential Suite is a real bonus as it consists of two adjoining double bedrooms separated by a sitting room.

The hotel offers three options for wedding receptions. The panoramic terrace room, **La Limonaia**, holds up to 110 guests and has both indoor and outdoor spaces with marvellous views across Rome. The main restaurant, **La Mirabelle**, holds up to 130 guests and has wonderful ceiling to floor windows that open out onto a charming terrace. The terrace itself seats up to 40, and offers you the perfect setting from which to gaze out across the Rome skyline and the gardens of *Villa Borghese*.

For smaller receptions a section of *La Mirabelle* can be separated from the main restaurant along with a private space on the terrace. All these rooms have an understated pale green and gold colour scheme set against an appropriately bridal white background. Menus here can be personalised, and the Maitre d' can help you arrange your hairdresser, beautician and limousines. As an additional endorsement this is also a popular venue for the locals, so you can be assured of style, service and excellent food.

Essential Information – Hotel Splendide Royal:

Availability:	Open all year	Organisation:	Receptions are organised by a small team of people, including the manager of the restaurant. Each wedding is planned individually, rather than as a package.
Size of party:	Up to 110	Entertainment:	A pianist or guitar accompaniment can be provided.
Children catered for:	Yes	Exclusivity:	It is highly unlikely that more than one reception would be held on the same day, although in this situation the events would be kept separate.

Prices from:		€115 per head	
Price Includes			
Venue Hire	✓	Centre pieces	✓
Staff	✓	Wedding cake	€5 supplement
Meal (four courses)	✓	Entertainment	✓
Aperitifs & Canapés	*		

* Depends on menu selection

Palazzo Ferrajoli €€€(€)

www.palazzoferrajoli.it

"We wandered from room to room in amazement… the space feels as though it could be a wing of the Louvre Museum with its high ceilings and ornate interiors".

Rome Wedding Guest

A beautiful old 17th century mansion, Palazzo Ferrajoli is a friendly and welcoming family residence with a past-guest list as impressive as its location on the famous Piazza Colonna. Although situated right in the very heart of Rome it couldn't be further from the madding crowd as, when the dark imposing doors are closed, the venue is enveloped in serenity. Formerly the Napoleonic French Embassy, the mansion is now a wonderfully warm and welcoming family home, and the owners pay a great deal of attention to the finer details of your wedding reception.

Entered via a red-carpeted stone staircase leading up from a charming private enclave just off Piazza Colonna, the rooms are filled with antique furnishings and many examples of fine art. The tall windows that look out onto the Piazza combine with the many mirrors and chandeliers to really make the most of the natural light. There are six dining rooms that look out onto Piazza Colonna across to the government buildings opposite; these rooms, each with a capacity of up to 50 guests, can either be combined to make one venue for up to 300, or hired separately in any combination for smaller parties. Each room is beautifully decorated, with elegant black and white tiled flooring throughout the rooms and a choice of colour schemes, from the red and gold corner room with its balcony over the Piazza, through combinations that include silver, turquoise, blue and pale gold.

This isn't a hotel so you won't be able to book rooms for your guests, but if you don't fancy trekking back to a hotel for your first night the venue also offers a single bridal suite, decked in red velvet and with a beautiful antique four-poster bed and Jacuzzi bathroom.

This very experienced venue has acquired many contacts and can help you arrange caterers, entertainment, transportation and all the services you need. The venue also has some charming private rooms which can be hired by special arrangement.

Essential Information – Palazzo Ferrajoli:

Availability:	Closed in August	Organisation:	Weddings will be organised by a small family team, the owners of the venue. Each wedding will be highly personalised.
Size of party:	Up to 300	Entertainment:	A pianist can be arranged, or couples can bring their own CDs. No loud music or dancing.
Children catered for:	Yes	Exclusivity:	Hire of the venue will be exclusive.

Prices from:	€70 per head for catering, approx €700 venue hire per room*		
Price Includes			
Venue Hire	✓	Centre pieces	*
Staff	*	Wedding cake	*
Meal	*	Entertainment	✓
Aperitifs & Canapés	*		

* Venue hire is €700 per room. Catering is additional and includes drinks, table decoration and wedding cake. Catering can be arranged according to most budgets in either a buffet or sit-down format, depending on the couple's specifications.

Grand Hotel Parco dei Principi €€€€
www.parcodeiprincipi.com

"It was the most elegant hotel I have ever stayed in. The overall atmosphere of the hotel made me feel like royalty."

Rome Visitor

This polished hotel is wonderfully friendly and refreshingly flexible when it comes to wedding receptions. Their service abounds with nice touches – the bride and groom can expect their first night room courtesy of the hotel, for example, and if table wine isn't your thing and you'd prefer to offer beer to your guests, you'll get your first round on the house.

The Winter Garden, Parco dei Principi

In addition to the extensive menu options, the hotel can tailor a menu to suit your budget and specifications. They can cater for the smallest of receptions up to the very largest (approximately 400), with an impressive selection of rooms to suit any size and, more importantly, any colour scheme as the hotel has a variety of beautifully decorated rooms. The most ideal of these is probably the Winter Garden, a square, frescoed room for up to 100 guests, lightly decorated in pink and cream, and surrounded by wide, ceiling to floor windows that open out onto a small terrace overlooking the hotel gardens. Additional rooms include the plush red and gold Sala Colonna, with its green velvet curtains and opulent gilt-edged mirrors, and the blue and gold Orsini & Farense, two bright rooms with numerous sparkling chandeliers and a small garden terrace. Welcome drinks and canapés can be served in the hotel gardens or by the pool at certain times of the year.

This venue is extremely flexible, with a pricing structure that allows you to tailor a reception to your budget, as the price per head typically includes just the five-course meal and venue hire. Any added extras come at a supplementary price, but the hotel can arrange most services, including welcome drinks and canapés, printed menus, flowers and entertainment.

Essential Information – Grand Hotel Parco dei Principi:

Availability:	Open all year	Organisation:	Receptions arranged by a small team of two people, who will also provide service on the day
Size of party:	Up to 400	Entertainment:	A disco can be held in the rooms on the lower level of the hotel, but these must be hired separately. Pianists and other musicians can be arranged by the hotel.
Children catered for:	Yes	Exclusivity:	On rare occasions, two weddings may be held on the same day, but these will be isolated to separate floors.

Prices from:	€105 per head*		
Price Includes			
Venue Hire	✓	Centre pieces	✓
Staff	✓	Wedding cake	✓
Meal	✓	Entertainment	✗
Aperitifs & Canapés	✗**		

*Alternative budgets can be catered for
**Price included in selected menus only

Ristorante El Toula €€€€
www.toula.it

"we held the rehearsal dinner at El Toula; they have a nice private dinning room for about 25 people, and the food and service are excellent".

Rome Mother-of-the-Groom

On a small, quiet piazza just a few minutes' walk from Via Condotti, the rather swish, designer street leading away from the Spanish Steps, El Toula is a charming restaurant well situated for Protestant weddings at All Saints' Church.

With its white vaulted ceilings and understated, light gold décor and pale, gleaming wood, the restaurant has a pleasantly private feel to it; conservative, but with extra polish and flair. The main restaurant provides a nice open, arched space for larger parties, whilst for groups of fewer than 20 a comfortable and homely private room is available (and although it unfortunately has no windows, it looks very atmospheric in flickering candle-light). This venue is smart but relaxed, with quiet, discreet service and quite a reputation for excellent food.

Essential Information – El Toula:

Availability:	Closed in August	Organisation:	Wedding receptions will be organised by the manager of the restaurant.
Size of party:	Up to 70	Entertainment:	A pianist can be arranged. Couples may also bring their own CDs.
Children catered for:	Yes	Exclusivity:	Exclusive hire of the restaurant is dependent on number of guests. There is separate room available for up to 20 guests.

Prices from:	€95 per head		
Price Includes			
Venue Hire	✓	Centre pieces	✗
Staff	✓	Wedding cake	✗
Meal	✓	Entertainment	✗
Aperitifs & Canapés	✗ (from €8)		

Druids Rock Pub €
www.druidspubrome.com/druids_rock/wedding_in_rome.htm

If you want a large party on a small budget and you're looking for a home-from-home, then the Druids Rock ticks all the boxes. Unlike all the other venues featured, at a basic level this venue will charge you nothing aside from the cost of whatever you drink. Of course you can't expect a five-star sit-down meal for this, but for large parties the manager will arrange a selection of sandwiches and a wedding cake, and at an extra cost (and with enough notice) can also provide evening entertainment. The staff here will also decorate the venue for you, or you are free to bring your own decorations.

Receptions are typically held in an open, upper level, but guests are free to use all areas of the pub, including the open area outside. The pub is situated next to the enormous church of Santa Maria Maggiore, and has a themed, wooden interior covered, as you would expect, with memorabilia and souvenirs from Ireland. And I can officially confirm that the Guinness isn't bad, either.

Essential Information – Druids Rock Pub:

Availability:	Open all year	**Organisation:**	Weddings receptions will be organised by the manager of the pub.
Size of party:	Up to 150, but not suitable for a small reception.	**Entertainment:**	A band can be arranged, but no dancing is permitted
Children catered for:	Yes	**Exclusivity:**	Exclusive hire an upstairs room. Use of the rest of the pub plus an outside area.

Prices from:	Variable, depending on number of drinks purchased.		
Price Includes			
Venue Hire	✓	**Centre pieces**	✗
Staff	✓	**Wedding cake**	✓
Meal	✓	**Entertainment**	✗
Aperitifs & Canapés	✗		

Other Recommended Hotels and Possible Reception Venues

Grand Hotel La Minerve ★ ★ ★ ★ ★ www.elegantsmallhotel.com/hotels/ eww333.html	**Il Castelletto ★** www.il-castelletto.com
Bernini Bristol ★ ★ ★ ★ www.berninibristol.com	**Residenze Cellini** www.residenzacellini.it
Boscolo Exedra ★ ★ ★ ★ ★ www.boscolohotels.com/hotel.cfm? SectionId=578	**Palazzo Brancaccio €€€€** www.palazzobrancaccio.com
Hotel Alimande Viale Vaticano ★ ★ ★	**Villa Giovanelli Fogaccia €€€€** www.villagiovanelli.it
Capo d'Africa ★ ★ ★ www.hotelcapodafrica.com	**Ara Pacis Restaurant La Capricciosa** www.arapacisrestaurant.it
Hotel Santa Maria ★ ★ ★ www.htlsantamaria.com	**Tullio** www.tullioristorante.it
Hotel Gladiatori ★ ★ ★ www.hotelgladiatori.it	**Le Grotte** 37 Via della Vite 06.0795336
Hotel Tirreno ★ ★ ★ www.hoteltirrenoroma.com	**L'avena e la Cartota** 5 Via dell'Acqua Santa 06.78358940
Hotel Quirinale www.hotelquirinale.it	

How to Get There and Around

Rome has two international airports: Fiumcino (Leonardo da Vinci Airport) situated approximately 30km from the centre of Rome, and Ciampino situated 15km from the centre of Rome. Shuttle buses run between both airports - see www.adr.it for information.

By car: I can't think of many reasons why anyone would choose to drive in Rome. It's the worst way to see the city, the traffic is terrible, conditions are dangerous and parking is impossible. If, for whatever reason, you need to have a car with you during your visit, make sure you know what routes you need to take and mug up on the etiquette here:
www.romebuddy.com/givesadvice/transport.html#driving
The usual car-hire companies can be found at both airports and routes to the centre of Rome are straightforward:
> **From Fiumcino** take the Rome-Fiumcino motorway to the centre of Rome
> **From Ciampino** take the Via Appia Nuova to the centre of Rome

By scooter: The coolest way to get around Rome is also the most fun, but you ought to have a bit of scooting experience before you try it. See page 55 for details of scooter-hire companies

By taxi: Official taxis in Rome are white or yellow with a lighted sign on top, and bear a yellow "Comune di Roma" shield on the side. You'd be well advised to stick to these, official taxis rather than take un-licensed ones in Rome - the Information desk at the airport will be able to direct you to the official taxi ranks. There is a fixed rate from both airports to anywhere in the city centre:
> **From Fiumcino** the rate is €60 (Fiumcino taxis) or €40 (Rome taxis)
> **From Ciampino** the rate is €30.
Be aware that elsewhere taxis may charge per passenger rather than by distance. In all cases, you're likely to be asked to pay a supplement for baggage.

By bus: Apart from providing another way to get to and from the airport, buses aren't the best way to get around Rome as they tend to be crowded and unpleasant to use. Better alternatives are trams (if you can work out the routes) or the wonderfully simple metro.
> **From Fiumcino** buses to Rome Termini Station run around every two hours and cost €9.
> **From Ciampino** the Terravision bus connects to low-cost airline flights and cost €7. See www.terravision.it
More information can be found at www.adr.it and www.atac.roma.it

By train: Rome's central station is Rome Termini (www.romatermini.it).
From Fiumcino take a non-stop train (Leonardo Express) to Termini from the airport station which is located directly opposite Arrivals. Trains leave every half hour and take approximately 35 minutes.
From Ciampino buses to Ciampino train station run every 30 minutes, take five minutes and cost €1. From Ciampino station you can take a train to Rome Termini
More information can be found at www.adr.it and www.trenitalia.com

By metro: Once you arrive in the city, Rome's metro network is an excellent way to get around and gives you good access to most of the major attractions, although there aren't nearly enough stations so you'll have to be prepared to do a fair bit of walking (blame those pesky archaeological ruins that get in the way every time they try to extend the network). Tickets can be purchased at the metro stations. For maps and timetables, go to www.metroroma.it

By tram: Trams and buses are both operated by ATAC but, on the whole, the trams are considered the easiest to use. A cheap and handy way to get around Rome above ground, they can nevertheless be somewhat difficult to navigate. Tickets need to be purchased at newsagents, not on the buses or trams themselves. More information can be found at www.atac.roma.it

©JoAnne Dunn Photographer

Local Information

Area Statistics for the Rome Region

	Average Sunlight (hrs)	Average Temperature		Heat & Humidity	Average precipitation (mm)	Wet days	Sunset times	
		Min	Max				Start of month	End of month
January	4	5	11	-	71	8	16.49	17.23
February	4	5	13	-	62	9	17.24	17.58
March	6	7	15	-	57	8	17.59	19.33
April	7	10	19	-	51	6	19.34	20.06
May	8	13	23	Moderate	46	5	20.08	20.37
June	9	17	25	Medium	15	1	20.38	20.49
July	11	20	30	Medium	15	1	20.48	20.29
August	10	20	30	Medium	21	2	20.28	19.45
September	8	17	26	Moderate	63	5	19.44	18.54
October	6	13	22	-	99	8	18.50	17.06
November	4	9	16	-	129	11	17.04	16.40
December	4	6	13	-	93	10	16.40	16.48

Source: Based on BBC Weather statistics for Rome

Public Holidays	
January	1st – New Year's Day 6th – Epiphany
March	Easter Weekend
April	(date depending on year)
May	1st – Labour Day
June	2nd – Anniversary of the Republic 29th – Sts Peter & Paul (Rome only)
August	15th – Assumption of the Virgin
November	1st – All Saints' Day
December	8th – Day of the Immaculate Conception 25th – Christmas Day 26th – Boxing Day

Checklist

The following is a checklist adapted from the one published in *The Wedding Planning Guide*. It is based on a twelve-month planning period, but these timescales are a guideline only and most can be adapted to give yourself more (or less) breathing space. Remember that different churches may well set different deadlines.

Twelve Months + to Go

Make the announcement to you friends and family that you are getting married abroad	
Decide on your planning method and start researching planning companies	
Agree on a budget	
Decide whether to have your honeymoon in the same location	
Arrange a preliminary trip to Rome if necessary	
If you are having a religious ceremony, make initial contact with your priest or minister	
Book your co-ordinator or tour operator	
Start looking at wedding dresses	
Make sure you both have valid passports	

Eleven Months to Go

Provisionally book your accommodation	
Provisionally book your reception venue	
Establish deadlines for paperwork requirements	
Start to research accommodation for your guests	
Begin searching for a photographer	
Start to research flights	
Consider ordering or making "Save The Date" cards	
Consider setting up a guest information website	
Start researching your honeymoon, if you are having one separately	
Decide on your guest list	

Ten Months to Go

Book your photographer	
Take out wedding insurance	
Book your flights as soon as you are confident of your wedding date to ensure best prices	
Put together your wedding information website if you are having one, including accommodation and logistical information.	
Book your honeymoon, if you are having one separately	
Pay any deposits	

Nine Months to Go

Send out your "Save the Date" Cards to warn people of your actual or approximate wedding date	
Start to think about your invitation designs	

Eight Months to Go

Start to think about your evening entertainment	
If you haven't already done so, make an appointment with your Local Registrar to Give Notice according to the Town Hall deadline (or if in the US, make an appointment with your local Italian consular office to make your *atto notorio)*	
Choose your witnesses and obtain copies of their passports	
Order any documents you may need to Give Notice (birth certificates, etc.), if this has not yet been done	
Make or order your wedding invitations	

Seven Months to Go

Begin to obtain quotes and make supplier bookings	

Six Months to Go

Give Notice to your local registrar, if you have not already done so.	
Start looking at suits for the men. Make reservations if necessary	
Order your wedding dress	
If in the US, make your *atto notorio* at your local Italian consular office	
If planning a wedding in Vatican City, begin the paperwork process	

Five Months to Go

Research guest excursions	
Make menu choices	
Start to shop for wedding rings	
Collect the Certificate of Authority from your local registrar	
Copy all legal documentation and courier to co-ordinator or consulate.	
Make sure all documentation has been submitted to the *anagrafe*	

Four Months to Go

As soon as your *Nulla Osta* has been granted, secure your civil venue booking	
Send your wedding invitations, along with an information pack or information website details	
Start to plan your hen night	
Make sure you have a confirmed booking for your hairdresser	
Make sure you have a confirmed booking for your florist	
Make sure you have a confirmed booking for your wedding cake	
Make sure you have a confirmed booking for your transportation	
Make sure you have a confirmed booking for your evening entertainment	
Organise your first dress fitting	
Construct your wedding gift list	

Three Months to Go

Finalise the guest list and send numbers to your co-ordinator or venue	
Make doctor's appointments for honeymoon jabs, if necessary	
Have your thank you letter templates ready for when your gift list opens	

Ten Weeks to Go

Confirm your menu and final numbers to your venue	
Buy gifts for your attendants	
Make your orders of the day / orders of service	

Nine Weeks to Go

Make your place settings and other paraphernalia, if necessary	

Eight Weeks to Go

Decide on how you will transport your dress and suits to the resort	

Seven Weeks to Go

Arrange your second dress fitting	

Six Weeks to Go

Finalise your table plan	

Five Weeks to Go

Make sure you are familiar with your suppliers' terms and conditions, and confirm how and when they want their balances paid	

Four Weeks to Go

Speak to your gift list holder to arrange delivery of gifts	
Make sure all the speeches are written	

Three Weeks to Go

Send your first batch of thank you letters	
Arrange to have your final dress fitting	

Two Weeks to Go

Order any currency you need (don't forget to include the money for balances)	

One Week to Go

Get your hair cut and your nails manicured	
Ship any paraphernalia to your venue	
Send your second batch of thank you letters	
Collect the suits	
Collect your currency (Euros)	
Make sure all details are finalised with your venue, co-ordinator and suppliers	

In Location

Pay all outstanding balances	
Go for your hair trial	
Confirm timings for the day	
GET MARRIED!	

After the Wedding

Obtain a copy of your marriage certificate from your co-ordinator or Town Hall	
Register your marriage with the GRO (General Registrar) on your return to the UK	
Send out your final batch of thank you letters	

--- **Area Contacts** ---

What follows is a variety of wedding-related suppliers based primarily in Rome. These have been taken either from personal recommendations or from local company directories.

Do bear in mind that some of the smaller companies (hairdressers and florists in particular) are unlikely to speak much English so it would be advantageous to book through a co-ordinator rather than tackling them directly unless you are fluent in Italian. Those companies that have specifically stated they have English-speaking employees have been marked with an (E) next to their phone number; you may also find English-speakers at the other suppliers, but you'd be advised to email or fax them first to establish a contact.

To conduct your own supplier searches, you can use online resources such as the Italian Yellow Pages, www.paginegialle.it/index.html, by entering the supplier type in "*Cosa*", and the location in "*Dove*". Remember to use the Italian city name (Roma), rather than the English version.

Town Halls & Churches/
Comuni e Chiesa

Rome Marriage Office

Ufficio Matrimoni
Via Petroselli 50
00186 Roma
Tel: +39 06 6170 3066
www.comuni.roma.it/info_cittadino
/schede/an_ma_03.htm

Campidoglio Wedding Hall

Palazzo Senatorio
Piazza del Campidoglio
00186 Roma

Caracalla Wedding Hall

Complesso di Vignola Mattei
Via di Valle delle Camene 2
00184 Roma

Villa Lais

Piazza G. Cagliero, 20
00181 Roma
Fax: +39 06 7839 1925
villalais@comune.roma.it
www.comune.roma.it

**Bascilica di San Pietro
(The Vatican)**

San Pietro (Cappella del Coro)
00120 Citta del Vaticano
www.vatican.va

**Chiesa di Santa Maria in
Aracoeli**

4 Piazza del Campidoglio, Roma
Tel: +39 679 8155

**Chiesa di Santa Maria in
Trastavere**

14/c Via della Paglia
Piazza Santa Maria
Trastavere, Roma

San Giorgio in Velabro

19 Via del Velabro
00186 Roma
Tel: +39 06 683 2930

San Bartolomeo all'Isola

22 Isola Tiberina
Piazza San Bartolomeo
Tiber Island
Tel: +39 06 687 7973

Sant'Andrea al Quirinale

29 Via del Quirinale
00187 Roma
Tel: +39 06 474 4801

Santa Maria in Cosmedin

80 Foro Trainano
Piazza Bocca delle Verita
Tel: +39 06 679 8013

Santa Sabina all'Aventino

1 Piazza Pietro d'Illiria
Tel: +39 06 574 3573

Santa Maria in Cosmedin

Piazza Bocca della Verta, 18
00186, Roma
Tel: +39 06 678 1419

Santi Giovanni e Paolo

Piazza San Giovanni e Paolo, 13
00185, Roma
Tel: +39 06 700 57 45

The Irish College

Via dei Santi Quattro, 1
00184 Roma
Tel: +39 06 772631 (E)
Fax: +39 06 7726 3323
reception@irishcollege.org
ufficio@irishcollege.org
www.irishcollege.org

San Silvestro in Capite
Piazza San Silvestro 00187 Roma Tel: +39 06 679 7775 Fax: +39 06 6979 9740 sansilvestro17@netscape.net www.freewebs.com/saintsilvester

St Patrick's Irish Church
Via Boncompagni, 31 00187 Roma Tel: +39 06 4203 1201 (E) Fax: +39 06 4203 1236 info@stpatricksrome.com www.stpatricksrome.com

Chiesa Santa Susanna
Via Venti Settembre, 14 00187, Roma Tel: +39 06 4201 4554 (E) Fax: +39 06 474 0236 rector@santasusanna,org www.santasusanna.org

Ogni Santi (All Saints' Protestant Church)
153/b Via del Babuino 00187 Roma Tel: +39 06 3600 1881 (E) www.allsaintsrome.org

Featured Reception Venues

St Regis Grand Hotel

Vittorio Emanuele Orlando, 3
Roma
weddings.grandrome@stregis.com
www.stregis.com/rome (E)

Hotel Forum Rome

Via Tor de'Conti, 25-30
00184 Roma
Tel: +39 06 679 2446 (E)
Fax: +39 06 678 6479
info@hotelforumrome.com
www.hotelforumrome.com

Hotel Splendide Royal

Via del Porta Pinciana, 14
00187 Roma
Tel: +39 06 421 689 (E)
Fax: +39 06 421 68800
splendide@splendideroyal.com
www.spendideroyal.com

Palazzo Ferrajoli

Piazza Colonna, 355
Roma
Tel: +39 06 692 00497 (E)
Fax: +39 06 692 00497
palferrajoli@tiscalinet.it
www.palazzoferrajoli.it

Grand Hotel Parco dei Principi

Via G. Frescobaldi, 5
00198 Roma
Tel: +39 06 854 421 (E)
Fax: +39 06 884 5104
principi@parcodeiprincipi.com
www.parcodeiprincipi.com

El Toula

Via della Lupa, 29
Roma
toula2@libero.it
www.toula.it
Tel: +39 06 687 3489 (E)
Fax: +39 06 687 1115

Druids Rock Pub

Piazza Esquilino, 1
Roma
Tel: +39 06 474 1326 (E)
thedruidspub@yahoo.it
www.druidspubrome.it

Wedding Co-ordinators

Weddings by Latour

Tel: +39 347 941 4667 (E)
www.weddings-by-latour.com
eletra@weddings-by-latour.com

Wedding in Rome

Tel: +39 06 439 0678 (E)
www.wedding-in-rome-com
lojacono@wedding-in-rome.com

Italia Celebrations

Tel: +39 333 483 9553 (E)
www.italiacelebrations.com
italiacelebrations@yahoo.com

Dolce Vita Weddings

Tel: +39 340 598 0936 (E)
Fax: +39 06 772 2168
www.dolcevitaweddings.com
info@dolcevitaweddings.com

Romolo Tours

Tel: +39 06 482 7258 (E)
Fax: +39 06 474 2509
romolotours@flashnet.it
www.weddingatstpeters.com

Marriage Italian Style

Via Fontana Mancina Snc,
Sacrofano, 00060 (RM)
Tel: +39 335 446 374 (E)
Tel: +39 06 908 2254
Fax: +39 06 908 2254
info@marriageitalianstyle.com
www.marriageitalianstyle.com

Rome at your Service

Via V.E. Orlando, 75
Rome, 00185
Tel: +39 06 484 583 (E)
Fax: +39 06 484 429
rays.srl@tin.it
www.weddingsinrome.com

Wed in Rome

47 Main Road
Naphill
High Wycombe
Bucks, HP14 4QD
info@wedinrome.co.uk
www.wedinrome.co.uk
Tel: +44 (0)1494 564205 (E)
Tel: +36 06 930 6933 (E)

The Book of Dreams

Tel: +39 081 532 12 23 (E)
info@thebookofdreams.net
www.thebookofdreams.net
Highly Recommended

By Cassini

90-100 Sydney Street
Chelsea
London
SW3 6NJ
Tel: +44 (0)790 387 9296 (E)
Tel: +39 347 799 3353 (E)
info@bycassini.com
www.bycassini.com

Exclusive Italy Weddings

Via Roma, 96
33033 Codroipo
Udine
Tel: +39 (0)432 913513 (E)
Fax: +39 (0)432 913809
info@exclusiveitalyweddings.com
www.exclusiveitalyweddings.com

Wedding Italy

Via de Gasperi, 6-8
33050 Gonars
Tel: +39 0432 931457 (E)
Fax: +39 0432 931196
mail@weddingitaly.com
www.weddingitaly.com

Photographers &
Videographers / Fotografo

JoAnne Dunn Photographer

47b, Via del Monte
84012 Angri (SA)
Tel: +39 081 947413 (E)
info@joannedunn.it
www.joannedunn.it
Highly Recommended

Alex Gritti

Via Pozzuoli, 7
Tel: 339 636 2266
studioflaminio@gmail.com
www.alexgritti.com

Rostaf

Via Marco V. Corvo, 10
Rome
Tel: +39 06 765 050
Fax: +39 06 761 0079
info@rostaf.it
www.rostaf.it

Foto Modica

Borgo Pio, 106
Rome
Tel: +39 06 686 7490
Fax: +39 06 6880 6008
fotomodica@hotmail.com

Fuoriquadro

Piazza Gondar, 15
Rome
Tel: +39 06 863 29578
info@fuoriquadro.it
http://fuoriquadro.it

Immagini di Paolo

V.le Trastavere, 249/A
Rome
Tel: +39 06 588 4245
paolo.ferracchiato@fastwebnet.it

Fotogioberti

Via Paolina, 5a
00184 Roma (S. Maria Maggiore)
Tel: +39 06 481 4755 / 488 2207
Fax: +39 06 4891 2455
Email: info@fotogioberti.it
www.fotogioberti.it

Imag1ne

Tel: +44 (0)7968 720983
info@imag1ne.com
www.imag1ne.com

Studio Luxardo

37 Via del Gambero
Rome
Tel: +39 066 79 4401 / +39 066
780 393

Foto Bellocchio

Via del Mascherino, 25
Rome
Tel: +39 06 686 5365
bellocchioluca@inwind.it

Claudio Filacchioni -
Photobrides

Photobrides, Rome
Tel: +39 063 550 8864
claudio.filacchioni@fastwebnet.it
www.photobrides.it

Camera Chiara

Via del Saracino, 20
Arezzo
Tel: +39 057 5370947
studio@camerachiara.com
www.camerachiara.net

Ladies' Hairdressers / Parrucchieri

Franco
Via Alessandro Volta, 18
Rome, 00153
Tel: +39 065 747 817

Marisa
Corso Vittorio Emanuele, 291
Rome, 00186
Tel: +39 066 861217

Ripetta 9
Via di Ripetta, 9
Rome, 00186
Tel: +39 063 610 390

Walter
Via G.G. Porro, 16
Rome, 00197
Tel: 39 068 084 695

Parrucchiere Grazia
Via Frattina, 75
Rome
Tel: 06 679 2046

AR Studio
Via Campo Marzio, 69
Rome, 00186
Tel: +39 066791495

Alternativa Hair Moda
Via XX Settembre, 4
Rome, 00187
Tel: +39 064885545

Carita Coiffeur
Corso Rinascimento, 6
Rome, 00186
Tel: +39 0668803698

Chez Mary
Via Santa Croce in Gerusalemme, 26a
Rome, 00186
Tel: +39 067028305

Sergio Russo
Piazza Mignanelli, 25
Piazza di Spagna
Rome, 00187
Tel: +39 (0)6 678 0457
Tel: +39 (0)6 678 1110

Studio 3
Piazza di Spagna, 51
Rome, 00187
Tel: +39 066791802
Tel: +39 068084104

Sergio Valente
Via Condotti, 10
Rome, 00187
Tel: +39 06 679 1268
Fax: +39 06 6704 0696

Roberto Carminati
Via Italo Svevo, 19
Rome 00139
Tel: +39 06 8713 7234
rcarminati@quipo.it
www.robertocarminati.com

Kami Noke
Via Fabio Numerio, 48-50
Rome, 00181
Tel: 39 06 785 0556
www.kaminoke.it

Noi Salon
Piazza del Popolo, 3
Rome, 00187
Tel: +39 06 3600 6284 (E)

Beauticians / Estetista

Aveda Salon
9 Rampa Mignanelli
Rome
Tel: +39 06 6992 4886
Tel: +39 06 6992 4257
Fax: +39 06 6978 0756
www.avedaroma.com

Marisa
Corso Vittorio Emanuele, 291
Rome, 00186
Tel: +39 066 861217

Ripetta 9
Via di Ripetta, 9
Rome, 00186
Tel: +39 063 610 390

Bruno e Massimo Necci
Via Frattina, 38
Rome, 00187
Tel: +39 066794516

Sergio Valente
Via Condotti, 10
Rome, 00187
Tel: +39 06 679 1268
Fax: +39 06 6704 0696

Jean Paul Troili Make-up Artist
Piazza SS Apostoli, 81
Rome, 00187
Tel: +39-06-6781486
Fax: +39-06-6790903

Beauty Planet
Via Veneto, 70
Rome, 00187
Tel: 06 4201 0865
Fax: 06 4787 1865

Wildwood Aesthetics Services
Vicolo Olivela, 36
Rome, 00041
Tel: +39 06 930 4942 (E)

Castelli
Via Condotti 22, Rome, 00187
Tel: +39 06 679 0998
parrucchieri@castelli-it.com
www.castelli-it.com

Compagnia della Bellezza
Via Gallia 70, Rome, 00183
Tel: +39 06 7045 0082
Fax: +39 06 7045 0082
www.compagniadellabellezza.it

L'Oasi del Benessere
Vicolo delle Grotte, 24
Rome, 00186
Tel: +39 06 6813 5559
Fax: +39 06 6813 5559
oasidelbenessere@yahoo.it
www.loasidelbenessere.com

Riccio Capriccio
Via Roberto de Nobili, 15
Rome, 00154
Via di S. Giovanni in Laterano,
202
Rome, 00184
Tel: +39 06 5160 0073
info@ricciocapriccio.com
www.ricciocapriccio.com

Speedy Beauty
Piazza B. Avanzini, 12
Rome, 00157
Tel: +39 06 4500 601 (E)
Fax: +39 06 4179 2063
speedybeauty@tiscalinet.it
www.speedybeauty.it

Warysan Club
Viale del Tintoretto, 100
Rome, 00142
Tel: +39 06 9727 7513
Fax: +39 06 972 5061
centribenessere@warysanclub.it
www.warysanclub.it

Men's Hairdressers / Parrucchieri per Uomo, Barbieri

Salone
Via Nomentana, 53
Rome

Chez Mary
Via Santa Croce in Gerusalemme, 26a
Rome, 00186
Tel: +39 067028305

Studio 3
Piazza di Spagna, 51
Rome, 00187
Tel: +39 066791802
Tel: +39 068084104

Il Capellaio di Quinto Bartoli
Lungotevere di Pietra Papa, 137
Rome, 00146
Tel: +39 065 599715

Look 2000
Via Basento, 17/19
Rome, 00198
Tel: +39 6 855 3145

Stirone
Via dei Pastini, 130
Rome, 00186
Tel: +39 06 679 4240

Uva
Via della Colonna Antonina, 25
Rome, 00186
Tel: +39 06 679 4139

Carbone
Via di S. Maria de' Calderari, 50
Rome, 00186
Tel: +39 06 687 9468

Privitello
Corso del Rinasciemento, 32
Rome, 00186
Tel: +39 06 687 9462

Gonnellini
Corso del Rinasciemento, 32
Rome, 00186
Tel: +39 06 6880 3123

Fedeli
Via Palermo, 21
Rome, 00184
Tel: +39 06 481 8067

Toni Al Parlamento
Via in Lucina, 10
Rome, 00186
Tel: +39 06 861 438

Maccari
Via in Lucina, 11
Rome, 00186
Tel: +39 06 687 1542

Di Giacomo
Via Genova, 25
Rome, 00184
Tel: +39 06 481 4254

Berretta
Piazza di S. Bernardo, 102/B
Rome, 00187
Tel: +39 06 488 5681

Barbarossa Enio
Via Torre Grotta, 129
Rome, 00132
Tel: +39 06 207 1667

Florists / Fioraio

Bocchi Fiori

136 Corso Vittorio Emanuele
00196 Rome
Tel: +39 668 90931
Fax: +39 668 892569

Via Domenico Chelini, 38
Tel: +39 680 78039
Fax: +39 6807 8042
Info@bocchifiori.it
www.bocchifiori.it

L'Arte del Fiore

Via Bella Villa, 55b
Rome
www.artedelfiore.it
Tel: 06 230 7013 / 347 702 5945

Marco Florarte

Via Palmiro Togliatti, 1448
Rome
marco.florarte@fastwebnet.it
www.marcoflorarte.it

Capoguzzi

Via Rodi, 13/15
Rome, 00195
Tel: +39 06 3974 2981

Manzone

Via Caverni Raffaele, 36/38
Rome, 00195
Tel: +39 06 3973 5438

Fulgenzi

Via Aldini Giovanni, 33
Rome, 00146
Tel: +39 06 557 2889

Fiore Proibito

Via di Boccea, 1115
Rome, 00166
Tel: +39 06 6190 1066

Tulipani Bianchi

Via dei Bergamaschi, 59
Tel: +39 06 87 5449

Pastor and Tjader

Via della Madonna dei Monti, 62/a
Tel: +39 06 478 222 232

Nuovo Concepto Floreal

Via dei Greci, 48
Tel: +39 06 4544 3923

Romano Fiori

Via Tomacelli, 20
Tel: +39 06 687 6145

Transportation

Wedding Day Cars & Limos / Auto da Ceremonia

Idea Limousines

Via E. Romagnoli
Rome
+39 349 442 7219
www.idealimousines.com

Limousine Services Rome

Tel: +39 338 742 5100 (E)
Tel: +39 334 379 4127
daytours@limoservicesrome.com
www.limoservicesrome.com

Rome Shuttle Limousines

Tel: +39 06 6196 9084
Fax: +39 06 6196 9085
info@romeshuttlelimousine.com
www.romeshuttlelimousine.com

Tourvisa Italia

Via Marghera, 32
Rome, 00152
Tel: +39 06 448 741
Fax: +39 06 445 6870
info@tourvisa.it
www.tourvisa.it

Bob's Limousines & Tours

Via A. Tamburlini 20
Rome, 00125
Tel: +39 06 575 6262 (E)
Fax: +39 339 651 6936
bob@romelimousines.com
www.romelimousines.com

UARA

Via Panisperna, 261
Rome, 00184
Tel: +39 06 679 2320
Tel: +39 06 679 8207
uara@isinet.it
www.limousineuara.com

Rome in Limo

Circonvallazione Ostiense, 183
Rome, 00154
Tel: +39 328 652 6705 (E)
Tel: +39 340 844 6292 (E)
Fax: +39 06 578 1399
info@romeinlimo.com
www.romeinlimo.com

Colosseum Travel

Tel: +39 06 5730 5406 (E)
Fax: +39 06 54 5900
www.colosseumtravel.com

Driver in Rome

Via Pian del Marmo, 21
Rome, 00166
Tel: +39 06 6152 2395
Fax: +39 06 6153 2259
info@driverinrome.com
www.driverinrome.com

Scooters / Motorina

Scooter Hire

Via Cavour, 80
Rome, 00184
Tel: +39 06 481 5669
Fax: +39 06 4543 5799
info@scooterhire.it
www.scooterhire.it

Trenoe Scooter

Piazza dei Cinquecento
Rome Termini
Tel/Fax: +39 06 4890 5823
rent@trenoescooter.191.it
www.trenoescooter.191.it

Happy Rent

Via Farini, 3
Tel: +39 06 481 8185

Scoot-a-long
Via Cavour, 302
Tel: +36 06 678 0206

Scooters for Rent
Via della Purificazione, 84
Tel: +36 06 488 5485

Taxis

Airport Connection Services
Tel: +39 06 338 3221

Co-operative Autoradiotaxi Romana 35-70
Tel: +39 06 3570

Pianeta Taxi 2000
Tel: +39 06 8822

Societa la Capitale Radio Taxi
Tel: +39 06 4994

Bakeries / Panetteria

Galligani Uliviero
Via Nomentana, 395/b
Rome
Tel: +39 06 823 254
www.galligani.it

Giolitti
Via Uffici del Vicario, 40
Rome
Tel: +39 06 699 1243
Fax: +39 06 6994 1758
info@giolitti.it
www.giolitti.it/home-e.html

Arnese
Via del Moro, 15/16
Rome, 00153
Tel: +39 06 581 7265

Cecere
Via B. Musolino, 45
Rome, 00153
Tel: +39 06 589 5014

Giovanni Riposat
Via delle Muratte, 8
Rome, 00187
Tel: +39 06 679 2866

Il Forno di Campo de'Fiori
Piazza Campo de' Fiori, 22/22a
Rome, 00186
Tel: +39 06 6880 6662

Cipriani
Via C. Botta, 19/23
Rome, 00184
Tel: +39 06 7045 3930

Innocenti
Via della Luce, 21a
Rome, 00153
Tel: +39 06 580 3926

Favours / Bomboniere & Confezioni

Faycram
Via Conca d'Oro, 331-335
Rome, 00141
Tel: +39 06 810 8612
Fax: +39 06 8838 4056
info@faycram.it
www.faycram.it

L'Angolo del Regalo
Circ.ne Gianicolense, 222
Rome, 00152
Tel: +39 06 5823 7736
langolodelregalolo@virgilio.it
www.langolodelregalo.it

Artigiana Dolciumi CDS
Via Santa Maria Goretti, 24
Rome, 00199
Tel: +39 0686218622

La Bottega del Cioccolato
Via Leonina, 82
Rome, 00184
Tel: +39 064821473

Moriondo & Gariglio
Via del Piè di Marmo, 21/22
Rome, 00186
Tel: +39 066990856

Musicians / Musicisti

Valentina Ducros (Vocalist)
info@valentinaducros.com
www.valentinaducros.com

Lorenzo Capelli (Pianist)
capelli@fastweb.it

Tastierista Maurizio (Vocalist)
Tel: +39 347 001 8068
info@maurypianobar.it
www.maurypianobar.it

Servizio DJ (DJ)
Tel: +39 393 288 9190
info@serviziodj.it
www.serviziodj.it

Deejay Rome (DJ)
+39 334 731 4943
info@deejayorganization.it
www.deejayorganization.it

Roma Servizi (DJs)
Tel (+39) 393 26 20 534
Fax: 06 4547 7517
mail@romaservizi.net
www.romaservizi.net

Max Guida (Vocalist)
max_guida@libero.it
www.maxguida.com

Lyric Soprano (Vocalist)
+39 338 806 2886
faba72@hotmail.com

Gagliardini (Band)
Alessia
marlu@tin.it

Tour Operators (offering weddings in Rome) / Agenti di Viaggi

Citalia
The Atrium London Road Crawley West Sussex RH10 9SR Tel: 0870 901 4013 italy@citalia.co.uk www.citalia.com

Cresta
Tel: 0870 238 7711 websales@bcttravelgroup.co.uk www.crestaholidays.co.uk

Kirker
4 Waterloo Court 10 Theed Street London SE1 8ST Tel: 0870 112 3333 Fax: 0870 066 0628 travel@kirkerholidays.com www.kirkerholidays.com

Magic of Italy
Magic Weddings King's Place 12-42 Wood Street Kingston-upon-Thames Surrey, KT1 1JF Tel: 0870 888 0228 www.magicofitaly.co.uk

Tourist Information / Turistica

APT Rome
Via Parigi, 11 Rome, 00185 Tel: +39 06 488991 Fax: +39 06 481 9316 info@aptroma.it www.romaturismo.com

ENIT
Via Marghera, 2/6 Rome, 00185 Tel: +39 06 49711 Fax: +39 06 446 3379 www.italiantouristboard.co.uk www.enit.it

Enjoy Rome
Via Marghera, 8a Rome, 00185 Tel: +39 06 445 1843 Fax: +39 06 445 0734 info@enjoyrome.com www.enjoyrome.com

Romebuddy
www.romebuddy.com

Angloinfo
http://rome.angloinfo.com/default.asp

In Rome Now
www.inromenow.com

Bibliography

Belford, Ros; Dunford, M; Woolfrey, C. *The Rough Guide to Italy.* London, England: Rough Guides, 2005.
Podesta, Gina. *A Romantic's Guide to Italy.* Berkeley, Canada: Ten Speed Press, 2004.
Rome Eyewitness Travel. London, England: Doring Kindersley Ltd, 1993

Online Sources
www.bbc.co.uk
www.britishembassy.gov.uk
www.clickbridal.com
www.comuni-italiani.it
www.confetti.co.uk
www.embitaly.org.uk
www.fco.gov.uk
www.fepqep.org
www.hitched.co.uk
www.imdb.com
www.intoitaly.it
www.italiansrus.com
www.italiantourism.com
www.italiantouristboard.co.uk
www.italyheaven.co.uk
www.italy-weddings.com
www.itconlond.org.uk
www.paginegialle.it
http://roma.katolsk.no/index.htm
www.romaonline.it/
www.romebuddy.com
www.siafitalia.org
www.sposi.it
www.theknot.com
www.tripadvisor.co.uk
www.vicariatusurbis.org/
www.virtualitalia.com
www.weddingchaos.co.uk
www.weddingguide.co.uk
www.weddings-abroad-guide.com
www.weddingsonline.ie

Acknowledgements

I would like to thank the following people for their assistance in helping me put this work together: all the hotels featured for their patience, help and professionalism; JoAnne Dunn and Camilla Cesarano for allowing me to use some of their wonderful photographs; James Beard for editorial help and advice; Claire Gould (aka *The Wedding Calligrapher*) for the beautiful map; the message board participants of Hitched, Confetti, Wedding Guide, The Knot, The Weddings Abroad Guide and Weddings Online and all the brides who have bombarded me with emails to tell me about their frustrations and give me plenty of ideas.

I'd also like to thank my husband James for making all those research trips far more romantic than they would otherwise have been. *Tu sei una stella!*

©JoAnne Dunn Photographer

Notes

9 781847 530707